CITIES
JERUSALEM

ABDO
Publishing Company

Nancy Furstinger

visit us at
www.abdopub.com

Published by ABDO Publishing Company, 4940 Viking Drive, Edina, Minnesota 55435.
Copyright © 2005 by Abdo Consulting Group, Inc. International copyrights reserved in all
countries. No part of this book may be reproduced in any form without written permission from
the publisher. The Checkerboard Library™ is a trademark and logo of ABDO Publishing
Company.

Printed in the United States.

Cover Photo: Corbis
Interior Photos: Corbis pp. 1, 5, 6-7, 10, 11, 14, 15, 16, 19, 20, 21, 23, 24, 25, 27, 28, 29;
    Getty Images p. 13

Series Coordinator: Jennifer R. Krueger
Editors: Heidi M. Dahmes, Megan M. Gunderson, Stephanie Hedlund
Art Direction & Maps: Neil Klinepier

Library of Congress Cataloging-in-Publication Data

Furstinger, Nancy.
    Jerusalem / Nancy Furstinger.
        p. cm. -- (Cities)
    Includes index.
    ISBN 1-59197-860-2
    1. Jerusalem--Juvenile literature. I. Title.

    DS109.9.F87 2005
    956.94'42--dc22
                                                              2004058362

CONTENTS

JERUSALEM

An ancient mapmaker once showed Jerusalem as the center of the world. Though it is not the center of the world, the city is central to world religion. Jerusalem is home to Christianity, **Islam**, and Judaism. So, it is often called the Holy City.

In 1000 BC, King David made Jerusalem his capital. Now, 3,000 years later, the city is Israel's capital. History springs alive in the walled Old City. This maze of winding streets is still known as "the navel of the world."

In the Old City, people are drawn to a holy wall and a prophet's footprint. The Old City is encircled by modern Jerusalem. Outside the walls, people visit a lifeless sea and a zoo filled with biblical creatures.

Jerusalem has seen a lot of conflict. It contains sites sacred to all three faiths. So, all three claim Jerusalem as their holy city. This has led to years of fighting. Today, Jerusalem's citizens are working to find peace.

Opposite Page: *Jerusalem is home to more than 692,000 people.*

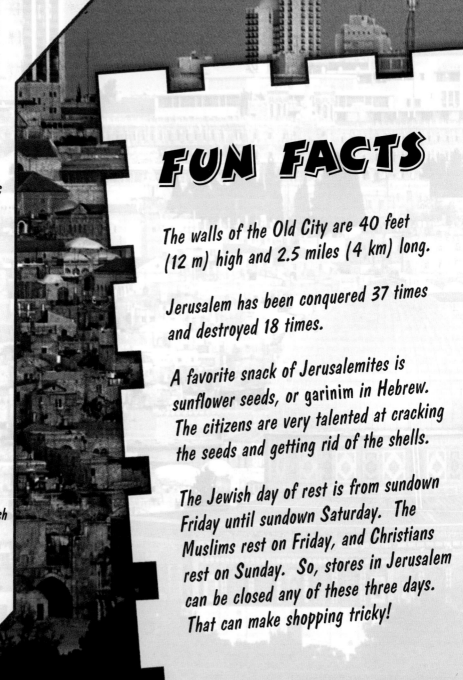

JERUSALEM AT A GLANCE

Date of Founding: About 2000 BC

Population: 692,300

Metro Area: 42 square miles
(109 sq km)

Average Temperatures:
- 50° Fahrenheit (10°C)
  in cold season
- 75° Fahrenheit (24°C)
  in warm season

Annual Rainfall: 20 inches (51 cm)

Elevation: 1,970–2,740 feet
(600–835 m)

Landmarks: Old City, Dead Sea

Money: Shekel

Languages: Hebrew, Arabic, English

FUN FACTS

The walls of the Old City are 40 feet (12 m) high and 2.5 miles (4 km) long.

Jerusalem has been conquered 37 times and destroyed 18 times.

A favorite snack of Jerusalemites is sunflower seeds, or garinim in Hebrew. The citizens are very talented at cracking the seeds and getting rid of the shells.

The Jewish day of rest is from sundown Friday until sundown Saturday. The Muslims rest on Friday, and Christians rest on Sunday. So, stores in Jerusalem can be closed any of these three days. That can make shopping tricky!

TIMELINE

1000 BC - King David names Jerusalem the capital of his Jewish kingdom.

586 BC - Babylonians conquer Israel.

63 BC - Roman soldiers conquer Jerusalem.

AD 1517–1917 - The Ottoman Empire controls Jerusalem.

1948 - Israel becomes an independent state on May 14; civil war begins and the city is split into East and West Jerusalem.

1967 - Jerusalem is reunified after the Six-Day War ends.

1980 - The Israeli Knesset declares Jerusalem the capital of Israel.

ANCIENT HISTORY

The area around present-day Jerusalem has been settled since the Stone Age. Around 10,000 BC, hunters settled in the region to grow crops and raise animals. Small farms dotted the plains. Then in 2000 BC, the Canaanite **culture** rose and formed cities.

The cities were part of a kingdom called Palestine. Jerusalem was one of these cities. The Philistines, Israelites, and Hebrews arrived in Palestine around 1200 BC. These peoples fought **civil wars** for control of the land. In 1020 BC, they were united by Saul, who then formed the country of Israel.

Saul died in a battle with the Philistines in 1000 BC. David then became king and defeated the **rebellion**. He named Jerusalem the capital of his Jewish kingdom. David brought the sacred **Ark of the Covenant** to Jerusalem, making it a holy city.

When King David died in 962 BC, his son Solomon began ruling. King Solomon expanded Jerusalem and built the First Temple to house the Ark of the Covenant.

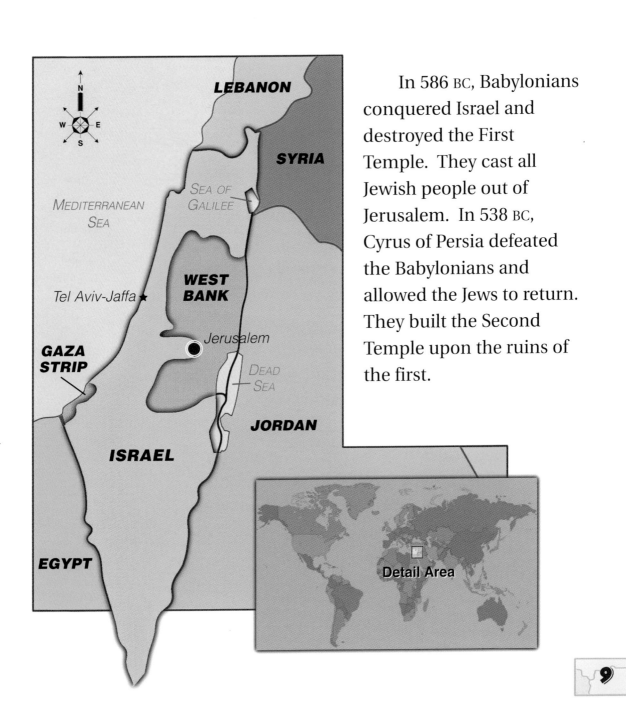

In 586 BC, Babylonians conquered Israel and destroyed the First Temple. They cast all Jewish people out of Jerusalem. In 538 BC, Cyrus of Persia defeated the Babylonians and allowed the Jews to return. They built the Second Temple upon the ruins of the first.

Detail Area

Other conquerors tried to wipe out the Jewish religion. They succeeded in burning the Second Temple, but the Holy City was always rebuilt. Then, Roman soldiers conquered Jerusalem in 63 BC. Catholicism slowly became the main religion of the Roman Empire.

During Roman rule, Jerusalem became a powerful and wealthy city. After the Roman Empire fell in AD 476, Jerusalem was conquered by a range of **cultures**.

During the **Crusades**, Christian armies fought Muslims for the right to rule. The Crusaders captured Jerusalem in 1099. However, the Muslim warrior Saladin regained the city in 1187.

The Muslim warrior Saladin

Later, Muslim soldiers called the Mamluks ruled from Egypt. They were conquered by the Ottomans in 1517. The Ottoman ruler, Suleyman the Magnificent, completed the stone walls around Jerusalem. After 1860, the growing city spread outside the safety of the walls.

The Ottoman rule lasted until 1917. During **World War I**, British troops captured Jerusalem. Jewish and Arab leaders argued about who was entitled to the land. Palestinian Arabs already living there claimed it as their own. But, Jewish **Zionists** wanted to return to the land of their ancestors.

Tensions between the Arabs and Jews increased. The British asked the **United Nations (UN)** to find a solution. In 1947, the UN planned to divide the city into two states. The Arabs declined, but the plan was passed anyway.

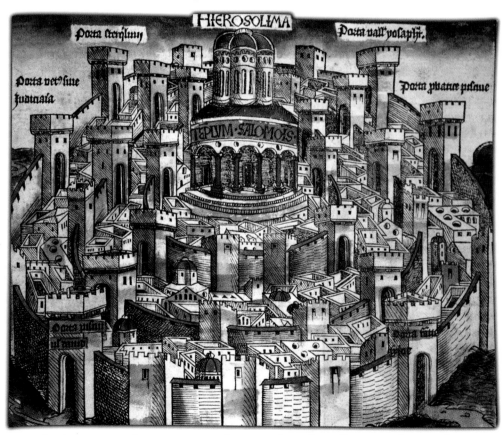

In the 1500s, eight gates were used to enter Jerusalem. To protect the city, these gates were closed from sunset to sunrise until the mid-1800s.

A DIVIDED CITY

On May 14, 1948, Israel became an independent state. When this was announced, war broke out. After the battle, Jerusalem was split in two. East Jerusalem went to Jordan, West Jerusalem to Israel. Despite the city's division, **Prime Minister** David Ben-Gurion declared West Jerusalem the capital of Israel.

East and West Jerusalem were reunified after the Six-Day War. The war ended in 1967, when the Israeli army captured East Jerusalem. Once the city was reunified, Israel's leaders discussed making Jerusalem the country's capital.

The **UN** disapproved of this idea. But the Israeli Knesset, or **parliament**, declared Jerusalem the capital of Israel in 1980. Jerusalem then became home to the Israeli government.

The 120-member Knesset meets near Jerusalem's Qiryat Ben-Gurion, which is the government complex. This complex is home to Israel's Supreme Court. However, not all government agencies are located in Jerusalem. The Ministry of Defense and several others meet in Tel Aviv-Jaffa.

Today, Jerusalem's 692,300 people are governed by an Israeli administration. Jerusalem's citizens are represented by a mayor and the municipal council. Elections for the council's 31 members are held every four years. The council then elects a mayor from its members.

In 2003, Uri Lupolianski became Jerusalem's mayor. He is the city's first ultra-Orthodox Jewish mayor. Lupolianski is studying Arabic so he can better communicate with Jerusalem's Palestinian citizens.

THE DEAD SEA

The Dead Sea is 1,312 feet (400 m) below sea level. There is no lower point on Earth.

The united Jerusalem covers 42 square miles (109 sq km). Much of the city stands on the Judean Hills. These hilltops overlook the Judean Desert.

Because Jerusalem is near the desert, summers are hot and dry. However, rain falls in winter. In all, the city only gets about 20 inches (51 cm) of rain a year. Every two or three years it even snows.

About 15 miles (24 km) east of Jerusalem is the Dead Sea. It earned this name because no animals live in its waters. However, the Dead Sea yields many other treasures.

The Dead Sea is nine times as salty as the ocean. This salt is mined and exported. Besides salt, minerals such as magnesium are harvested from the Dead Sea. The mineral waters aid healing, so spas are found along its shore.

Caves high above the sea sheltered the Dead Sea Scrolls. These ancient texts date back to 200 BC. They were found by a shepherd in AD 1947. The texts offer glimpses into the Bible and daily life of Palestine.

The Ein Gedi Spa is located near Jerusalem and the Dead Sea. This spa has several swimming pools that are filled with healing mineral waters.

AROUND TOWN

Many small shops and markets line Jerusalem's streets.

In Jerusalem, some people work in factories. They make chemicals, **textiles**, shoes, pencils, and plastic products. Others work in the diamond-cutting and jewelry industries. But many citizens of Jerusalem work in the service trades, especially tourism.

Tourists from around the world flock to Jerusalem. Most head to the Old City, in the heart of modern Jerusalem. Here, bazaars called souks offer local crafts. Shoppers must bargain with merchants to arrive at a fair price. They buy lucky charms, **menorahs**, dresses, rugs, and glass.

Other tourists combine shopping with business. The city hosts international conventions, meetings, exhibitions, and fairs. However, most tourists come to the city while on a journey to a holy place. This journey is called a pilgrimage.

Getting to the holy sites in Jerusalem can be tricky. In the mid-1970s, more roads were built in Jerusalem. However, traffic problems remain. Many of the streets are too narrow for cars, and there are rarely road signs!

Many Jerusalemites walk or use pushcarts to get around the city. Buses and taxis called *sheruts* offer public transportation as well. Most tourists enter the city through the Jerusalem Airport.

ANOTHER INDUSTRY

Many Israelis head to the outskirts of Jerusalem to volunteer at a kibbutz. A kibbutz is a self-sufficient farming village where residents live and work in a commune. Kibbutzniks own the property and share the work and any profits from that work. They might pick citrus fruits, watch young children, or make crafts.

JERUSALEMITES

Since Jerusalem is a holy city, most of its citizens are very religious. Most Jerusalemites are Jewish. Muslims and Christians make up the rest of the population.

Religion is a huge part of Jerusalem's **culture**. It determines the language spoken. Hebrew is the language of the Jewish citizens. Muslims speak Arabic. However, many citizens speak both of these languages and English.

Food in Jerusalem is also influenced by religion. Across the city, **kosher** restaurants follow strict rules. Jewish law forbids meat and dairy products to be eaten in the same meal. Certain meats or fish cannot be served either. Both Jews and Muslims are forbidden to eat pork.

During Passover, Jews do not eat anything with leaven, or yeast. Instead they eat matzo, which is brittle, flat bread. This is a reminder of when the Israelites fled Egypt and slavery in the 1200s BC. They had no time to wait for their bread to rise.

Opposite Page: A young Jerusalemite enjoys a falafel pita.

FOOD FOR THOUGHT

Jerusalemites eat many foods. Round, flat bread called pita is used to scoop up spicy dips such as tahini, a sesame seed paste. Moroccan cigars, which contain minced meat rolled in pastry and fried, are also enjoyed.

Street vendors stuff pita with falafel, which is deep-fried chickpea balls. They grill kebabs of spicy meat on a skewer. Fresh fruits are available, too. For dessert, Jerusalem kugel is a baked noodle pudding served with pickles!

19

Throughout Jerusalem, schools are also separated by language. In this school, students are taught in Armenian.

Modern Jerusalem surrounds the Old City. Jerusalem's boundaries continue to expand. Throughout the city, apartment buildings and row houses crowd narrow alleyways.

Visiting the neighborhood of *Me'a She'arim* is like stepping back into Eastern Europe during the 1700s. Instead of Hebrew, Orthodox Jews speak Yiddish. And men wear traditional black coats, while women wear scarves or wigs and long dresses.

Religion even influences education in Jerusalem. Israeli children must attend school from ages 5 to 15. Jewish elementary and secondary schools teach in Hebrew. Arab schools teach in Arabic. After secondary school, students may attend a university.

Students of any religion can enroll at Hebrew University. It contains Israel's national library. Hadassah University Medical Center is in western Jerusalem. Medical students study at this world-renowned hospital. Students of the arts attend the Bezalel Academy of Arts and Design.

Hebrew University was founded in 1925.

HOLIDAYS

Whether a Jew, Christian, or Muslim, most in the Holy City celebrate religious holidays. For Jews, Rosh Hashanah begins the New Year in September or October. The ten days following Rosh Hashanah are days of prayer.

The days of prayer end with Yom Kippur, the holiest day. It is called the Day of Atonement. On this day, Jews pray for God's forgiveness. The Jewish Feast of Lights, Hanukkah, is celebrated in December. For eight nights, candles in a **menorah** are lit.

A special Christian holiday is held on December 24. During Christmas Eve, people journey to nearby Bethlehem for Midnight Mass. The Mass is held at the Church of the Nativity, Jesus Christ's birthplace.

In spring, another holiday takes place at the Church of the Holy Sepulchre. Here, Greek Orthodox Easter is observed with the Holy Fire. During this time, Jews celebrate Passover. It marks when the prophet Moses led the Israelites out of Egypt.

Families often celebrate Passover by re-enacting the Israelites' journey out of Egypt.

Muslims celebrate Ramadan during the ninth month of the **Islamic** year. They pray and fast. Nothing is eaten between sunrise and sunset during that month. However, Muslims are allowed to eat one meal after dark. The end of Ramadan is marked by Eid al-Fitr, a celebration feast.

THE OLD CITY

One of the biggest destinations for pilgrims is the Old City of Jerusalem. There, tourists can walk in the footsteps of biblical figures. The Old City has been divided into the Muslim, Armenian, Christian, and Jewish quarters.

In the Muslim quarter, the golden Dome of the Rock glitters. This Muslim shrine was completed in AD 691, and it is decorated with Persian tiles. It contains a rock with the Muslim prophet Muhammad's footprint. Muslims believe it was from that spot that Muhammad rose to heaven.

The Dome of the Rock

In the Armenian quarter, the Cathedral of St. James is the focal point. Legend says that the grave of the apostle Saint James the Great rests here.

In the Christian quarter, the Church of the Holy Sepulchre is found. This site is thought to be where Jesus Christ died, was buried, and rose again. *Via Dolorosa*, or the Street of Sorrows, is the route Christ walked to his death. Pilgrims retrace his path, following the 14 stations of the cross to the church.

The Western Wall is a holy place that is popular with tourists of all religions.

In the Jewish quarter, the Western Wall is all that remains of the Second Temple. Jews have been worshipping at the wall since the Romans destroyed it in AD 70. Cracks in the stone blocks hold written prayers. Today, Orthodox Jews still pray in the plaza.

MUSEUMS TO SEE

Outside the Old City, Jerusalem is full of sites to visit. At the Israel Museum, a feast of many **cultures** can be enjoyed. The collection features treasures dating back to 1.5 million BC.

The Israel Museum has several buildings containing exhibits. In one, a cavelike dome holds the Dead Sea Scrolls. In another, paintings by Russian-Jewish artist Marc Chagall are displayed. The Billy Rose Art Garden holds sculptures. Classes in drawing, sculpture, and photography are given in the Ruth Youth Wing.

Many people visit Yad Vashem. Its name means "a monument and a name." This site serves as a memorial for the more than 6 million Jews killed in the **Holocaust** during **World War II**.

One museum at Yad Vashem features artwork from people in the death camps. Another contains photographs, records, and personal items of those who perished. The Children's Memorial flickers with thousands of reflected candles that honor the 1.5 million children who died.

Hope blooms at Yad Vashem's Avenue of the Righteous Among the Nations. There, 2,000 trees honor non-Jews who risked their lives to save Jews. A plaque displays the name of the person each tree is honoring. Eighteen thousand more heroes are honored in other plaques throughout the avenue.

The Dead Sea Scrolls are found in the Book of the Shrine, one of the Israel Museum's many buildings.

KEEPING BUSY

Jerusalemites often begin playing soccer as children.

Today, soccer is Israel's national pastime. From October to May, seats fill up at Teddy Stadium. Two teams from Jerusalem, Beitar Jerusalem and HaPoel, play matches here. The stadium seats up to 20,000 fans who chant and blow horns.

Basketball is the second-most popular sport. Amateur basketball leagues play pickup games in city parks. Jerusalem's professional team, Hapoel, plays at the Goldberg Sports Hall.

Outdoor activities are also unbeatable. The Society for the Protection of Nature in Israel leads hikes. Budding **archaeologists** can get their hands dirty at a Dig for a Day program.

Another way to keep in shape is folk dancing. Community centers offer lessons every night except Friday. Basic steps are in a different order for each song. Most dances, such as the *hora*, take place in a friendly circle.

A hike through the Jerusalem Biblical Zoo lets visitors see many animals mentioned in the Bible. Lions, fallow deer, oryx, cheetahs, and crocodiles live in this zoo. **Endangered** species such as the golden lion tamarin also dwell there. In the Holy City, the spirit of Jerusalem continues to captivate.

The leopard is one of the many animals found in the Jerusalem Biblical Zoo.

GLOSSARY

archaeologist - one who studies the remains of people and activities from ancient times.

Ark of the Covenant - a chest that held the tablets of the Ten Commandments.

civil war - a war between groups in the same country.

Crusades - Christian holy wars fought from the 1000s to 1200s to reclaim the Holy Land from the Muslims.

culture - the customs, arts, and tools of a nation or people at a certain time.

endangered - in danger of becoming extinct.

Holocaust - the killing of 6 million Jewish people, and many other prisoners, by Nazi forces during World War II.

Islam - the religion of Muslims. It is based on the teachings of Allah through the prophet Muhammad as they appear in the Koran.

kosher - selling or serving food that is prepared according to Jewish law.

menorah - a candlestick stand with 7 or 9 branches lit during Hanukkah.

parliament - the highest lawmaking body of some governments.

prime minister - the highest-ranked member of some governments.

rebellion - an armed resistance or defiance of a government.

textile - of or having to do with the designing, manufacturing, or producing of woven fabric.

United Nations (UN) - a group of nations formed in 1945. Its goals are peace, human rights, security, and social and economic development.

World War I - from 1914 to 1918, fought in Europe. Great Britain, France, Russia, the United States, and their allies were on one side. Germany, Austria-Hungary, and their allies were on the other side.

World War II - from 1939 to 1945, fought in Europe, Asia, and Africa. Great Britain, France, the United States, the Soviet Union, and their allies were on one side. Germany, Italy, Japan, and their allies were on the other side.

Zionist - of or relating to a movement to restore a Jewish homeland in Palestine.

SAYING IT

David Ben-Gurion – DAY-vuhd behn-gur-YAWN
Knesset – KNEHS-eht
matzo – MAHT-suh
souk – SOOK
Suleyman – soo-lay-MAHN

WEB SITES

To learn more about Jerusalem, visit ABDO Publishing Company on the World Wide Web at **www.abdopub.com**. Web sites about Jerusalem are featured on our Book Links page. These links are routinely monitored and updated to provide the most current information available.

INDEX